A Father's Playbook

How I Won Child Custody

By David Morefield

I would like to thank Karen, My Mom,
Bradley, Sean, Jennifer, George, Linda,
Travis, Tony, O'Brien, Ray and Chris for
their unwavering support
in this fight.

Table of Contents

Introduction

"Behold, I send you forth as sheep in the midst of

wolves: be ye therefore wise as serpents, and

harmless as doves."

- Matthew 10:16, King James Version, The Bible

I am a single father. At the age of 21, I had a son while I was still in college. My son's mother was threatening to get an abortion unless I married her, so I didn't think I had much of a choice. The day we got married at the courthouse, she said, "Now I own your ass!" and that was the beginning of the next 18 years of hell in my life.

Although we were only married for a short time and it was one of the worst experiences of my adult life, I have learned a lot along the way. The only good thing that came out of our marriage was my son. I was young and stupid; of course, I thought I knew it all. Man, was I in for a ride.

Once I was divorced, I was under the impression everyone would act in my son's best interests and just follow the court order. Again, I was young, naïve and foolish. This was going to be a journey that not only took its toll on me, but on my son as well.

In the years following our divorce, my ex-wife dictated everything to me, and I begrudgingly accepted it. I was threatened with not seeing my child. She used threats and intimidation to run my life, and I allowed it. There were many times when I was supposed to get visitation with my son and on a whim she would decide I would not be able to see him.

I felt she was completely in control: And she was. I would compromise to keep a relative peace and then attempt to renegotiate. Despite my best efforts and intentions, this only empowered my ex-wife to further try to control my life. She constantly threatened to take me back to court and would call me sometimes 20 to 30 times a day to harass me. I even got written up at a job because "my personal life was interfering with the office." My ex-wife called the company's main number repeatedly and was harassing the receptionist because I would not answer my cell phone. Not cool at all. I felt like my life was out of control and there was little I could do about it.

I have chosen to own my mistakes and share my story in the hopes that you will learn from my failures. There is no reason to sugarcoat anything: My intent is to be as open and honest as possible.

As my son grew older, he saw me less frequently, and when I would call, my ex-wife would not allow me to speak to him unless I agreed to concede to some demand she was making. It seemed every conversation quickly became a negotiation. I was being expected to make deals with the devil to get what the court had already ordered.

For example, while I was serving overseas on a 6-month deployment as a private military contractor, I called my ex-wife and asked to speak with our son. She told me he didn't even know who I was and that he did not want to talk to me. Then my ex-wife told me she was going to change his last name to her new husband's last name; she also said her new husband was going to adopt my son. Once again, she refused to let me speak with my son, and I hung up on her. She promptly called me back on my Middle Eastern mobile phone and started telling me how stupid I was for not blocking my number this time because now she "could call anytime she wanted." I let her ramble, rant and rave as long as she wanted; after all, she was calling me internationally and my incoming calls were free. I felt the situation was hopeless, and I was not sure what to do.

This power struggle continued for years, and my inaction enabled my ex-wife to essentially control my life. I could not make plans for my son and I to do something like go camping on a weekend because she would cancel the visitation at the last minute. I couldn't make plans to go out of town with my son to see family without her demanding that I agree to some sort of arrangement where I would give up more visitation.

Planning Christmas and Thanksgiving with family was

very stressful because my ex-wife would threaten to

withhold visitation in exchange for something that

would just benefit her. At no time did my ex-wife ever

seem concerned about what was best for my son: it

seemed she was just using him a pawn to gain control

of me and the rest of my family.

Do you remember Faustus, the character who

made a deal with the devil? Every time I compromised

with my ex-wife, I felt violated. I was always on the

losing end of the deal. It was as if I was Faustus selling

my soul on a lie. She was incapable of keeping her

word, and she would swear later she never had agreed

to something, or would change the terms of the

agreement after the fact. There seemed to be no end

in sight.

It seemed that no matter what, I was pretty much screwed. To be honest, I was frustrated and angry about the situation. This lingering frustration affected me mentally, physically and spiritually. It was like a cancer eating at my soul. My son was not getting a proper education, was being moved around all the time, and I was not able to spend any time with him.

In addition to this, my son's everyday life living with his mother was taking an emotional toll on him. This had to change, but how?

On several occasions during the time I had been working as a private military contractor, I had faced the prospect of being killed. I also had a lot of time to analyze my life and cogitate about how I wanted to live out the rest of my days as well as what I wanted out of life. These experiences brought me to the realization that I needed to stop acting like Neville Chamberlain and become more like Winston Churchill.

In 1938, Neville Chamberlain was the prime minister of the United Kingdom. Chamberlain met with Hitler and made a deal known as the Munich Agreement that gave the Sudetenland to Germany and left Czechoslovakia virtually defenseless. Upon his return to England, Chamberlain declared that the Munich Agreement meant "Peace in our Time." As we all know, not long after this agreement Hitler continued his push across Europe. The policy of appeasement does not work well when dealing with some people; they will view it as weakness, and it will only encourage their poor behavior.

Sir Winston Churchill replaced Chamberlain and established himself as an unwavering leader in the face of crisis. Churchill was quoted as saying, "If you're going through hell, keep going." He kept his cool under the mounting pressure of the German aggression and ultimately led the United Kingdom through some of its worst times of World War II.

In plain English, "Stop being a capitulating coward and stand up for my son, no matter what the cost." How was it that I could get shot at and keep my wits about me, but the minute I am threatened with further litigation I would back off? I was being a complete coward and allowing fear to dictate my response. I kept hearing from others that it was impossible for a father to get custody of his child unless the mother was in prison and I let this dampen my spirit. I accepted defeat before I even took up arms.

I am honestly grateful that nobody revoked my man-card for lying down like that. While I am tempted to be full of guilt and shame for not taking action sooner, I chose to make a radical change moving forward; no sense punishing myself for the past.

I realized my willingness to negotiate and compromise had gradually become a weakness and I was being abused.

Why do I tell you these things? Well, that is simple: They happened to me because I was stupid and allowed it to happen. Also, I am hoping you will hear my story and avoid repeating my failures. It would bring greater meaning to everything I have endured if others learn from my many mistakes.

I thought about fighting for custody many times before actually pulling the trigger, and I wondered, "How hard it could be?" After all, I was a sane man with a clean record. I also had good intent for my son's life and wellbeing. My ex-wife lived a life full of instability and complete chaos. She couldn't hold a job, maintain a place of residence for any given amount of time and was constantly battling everyone in her life. My son had been in five schools in five years; he was way behind academically, as well as socially. When I filed a motion to modify child custody, my son was not even enrolled in an accredited school, and he had been instructed to lie to me about where he was attending classes.

The big question was, "How hard would it be for other people to see this?" The answer I have come to is quite simple: Many people will side with the mother, including the courts. It didn't matter what had

happened: If I did not have some irrefutable evidence,

nothing would have ever changed. Even with evidence,

there were times the court, state services or others still

gave the benefit of the doubt to my son's mom.

This was a hard fight, and things did not always

go as planned. But that's life. Life is not fair. Court

sucks. Nobody is going to lead you by the hand. You

must be willing to accept many defeats on your path to

victory. There will be casualties. My physical health is

a good example.

As I was planning my strategy, I wrote out a set

of rules of engagement for myself to follow so in the

thick of the tumultuous battles that lay ahead, I would

already have a predetermined response. Think of it as

contingency planning for war and then you'll find the

right mindset for this kind of thought. This strategy

was in no way complete at the beginning of the battle,

but as the war raged on, I was able to develop it into a

set of guidelines I wish I would have possessed years

ago.

The purpose of writing this book is to share my

story, thoughts and experiences with other single dads.

I wish I had had the words contained here at the very

beginning; I think it would have helped me avoid the

mistakes I made.

This book is not to give you legal advice and

should not be used in the place of competent legal

counsel. Your attorney went to law school and knows

the law; that is not in question. But the truth is it

doesn't matter who your attorney is: The outcome of

the case rests on YOU.

I have had many lengthy conversations with other fathers who have asked me, "How did you get custody of your son?" Answering this question over and over again, I decided I should write a book.

It seems family courts in every state have a natural tendency to lean towards the mother. This is something I challenge you to accept; don't fight it. This is not something you are likely to change or influence on your own. Focus your attention only on your case and what is best for your child and let the rest of the world do its thing. Be the exception to the rule.

My prayer is that this book will empower single fathers to stand up for their children and do what is in the best interest of those children. When it is necessary to get custody of your child, I wish you the best. When it is not necessary to fight on your child's behalf, I hope you will stand down and find an alternate solution.

I would also ask that any single father reading this book would read the first chapter and then give themselves at least a weekend to think about it before committing to further legal action. While a custody battle is warranted in some cases, many times it is not the best approach and should be avoided, much like combat. Please take Chapter One to heart and do some serious soul searching and forward thinking before jumping head first into all-out combat. Hasty actions have consequences. Only you, with the help of your closest circle of friends, are going to be able to accurately assess your specific situation.

For those with no clear choice but to fight it out in court, never ever give up. Once you have retained legal counsel, I strongly urge you to rely on your attorney's advice and follow their instructions. If you and your attorney are not walking in the same direction, you cannot fight together against an enemy force. You are paying your attorney for their counsel, but it is up to you to follow their direction. The outcome of your case rests more on you than anyone else in the equation, so keep that in mind as you start planning and defining your future actions.

Chapter 1 – The Point of No Return

"The supreme art of war is to subdue the enemy without fighting." – **Sun Tzu, The Art of War**

Before deciding to file for custody of your child, I would encourage you to learn about the process and what is involved. Then you must be honest and answer some very tough questions for yourself.

1. Am I sure that there is no alternative aside from fighting a custody battle?
2. Does the benefit to my child/children, outweigh the risks to myself and to their welfare?
3. Am I totally committed?
4. Am I prepared to lose everything I have, including my own freedom, if I pursue custody?

5. Do I have the undying support of my family and friends?

If and only if you have answered "yes" to the above questions should you even entertain fighting for custody. Besides the obvious financial challenges of being in a prolonged custody battle, I have endured some of the most heartbreaking experiences a father can imagine. At one point, my ex-wife manipulated my son to tell the police at school that I was physically abusive. The police questioned me for hours, and at the end of the meeting, my son chose to go home with me; but my heart was wounded that my son could ever do something like that to me. I will speak more about this later. Had things gone south, I could have been arrested and lost my freedom; my life would have been changed forever.

There have been many times when I have walked into the room and everyone was talking about how I was an abusive, wife beating, child abusing, murderer – yet nobody truly knew anything about me, except what my ex-wife told them. This is not unique to my situation. I will address this and how to deal with it later.

Oh, how close I have come to being arrested based on just my ex-wife's allegations. Thankfully, the police have done their jobs and have investigated her claims. But, in this country, there is no such thing as proven innocent; be happy with a ruling that there is not sufficient evidence to file charges – that's about as good as it is going to be.

Why has my ex-wife not been charged for her false reports? Why is she not committed to a mental health institution? The answer is crystal clear: Life is not fair. Accept it and move forward. Do all you can for your child, keep your life clean and let God handle the rest.

"What is God going to do for me?" you might ask. Well, I would tell you I am not sure where we would be today without a lot of time in prayer and the support of my family, friends and my church.

Family court is like a knife fight – Nobody really wins and everyone is going to bleed, especially your children. This is why I strongly urge anyone planning to fight for custody to exhaust all avenues before choosing to go down this road.

In actual combat, you risk your life, and it is utterly terrifying. In the combat of the family court system, it might be a different kind of risk, but it still has long-term consequences. The big difference for me was that in the family courts, it was not just myself who was at risk, but also my child's future. If you are like me and value your child/children over yourself, watching them get wounded repeatedly along the way is extremely taxing to the soul; suffering a wound at their hands is even more heartbreaking.

You might say, "But wait, you won. You got custody of your son. Why are you saying this?" Yeah, I got custody of my son, but I would not have pursued this path unless I truly believed it was absolutely necessary and our only option. My son has been through hell, and it will likely leave some marks on his life for a long time, but he is growing stronger every day and I am proud to see him succeeding in his pursuits.

This past summer, my son and I went on a tour of Germany and Austria. I listened with pride as my son translated for me and demonstrated his mastery of the German language. That is something no one will ever be able to take away from us.

Now my son has graduated and is headed to college in the fall. His mother has no choice but to beg for his attention because she has no power over him or me. She will likely spend the rest of her days trying to understand why our son will have nothing to do with her. Unfortunately, she still does not see where she has ever wronged him or me. That is her onion to peel.

It is my prayer that your story also arrives to the point where you have a wonderful relationship with your child/children. In my case, it has made all of the heartache, financial loss and legal risk completely

worth it.

Chapter 2 – Planning for Success

"Victorious warriors win first and then go to war, while defeated warriors go to war first and then seek to win."

– Sun Tzu, The Art of War

On the battlefield, generals define the rules of engagement to dictate the conduct expected by a soldier. Likewise, you should define your rules of engagement prior to coming into contact with your adversary. Yes, I said adversary. You will need to compromise at times and always conduct yourself in a respectful manner toward the other party, but never lose sight of the fact that they are your adversary in this battle.

You are not just the general, but you are also the grunt serving on the front lines. You are an army of one. Your actions will have the most impact on the outcome of this battle. You must include your legal counsel in this process and make sure they are onboard with all of your plans. You will be in a partnership with your legal counsel and you need to be in agreement as you define a direction to follow. But, make no mistake: Your actions or lack thereof will follow you forever.

Holding yourself to these rules can help during times of great stress. When you are unable to critically think about what you need to do next, fall back on the rules you have outlined and you will be much better off. This takes discipline, prior planning and a whole lot of patience.

I remember taking some time away from everyone and defining some of the rules that would govern my actions and words moving forward in regard

to my ex-wife and my son. Some of these rules I

adopted from the teachings of Sun Tzu's Art of War

and some from other military strategies I have studied.

After all, if you are planning a battle, why not look at

the strategies that have worked for centuries on the

battlefield and adapt them to your circumstances? I

have also included some others I learned through trial

and error.

I have broken the list down into two categories:

Those regarding how I was to conduct myself with my

son's mother; and how to conduct myself with

everyone else, especially my son Caleb.

Chapter 3 – Rules of Engagement for Dealing with the Ex

When defining these rules, I tried to place myself in the judge's seat and see things through his/her eyes. The only way I could see possibly gaining custody of my son and successfully defending custody was to differentiate myself from my son's mother. This meant containing my anger, being outwardly non-reactive and often times relying on my attorney to speak on my behalf.

These simple words of self-guidance were honestly very difficult for me to follow at times, but when I failed to follow them, I got burned. If you feel like you are being punched in the face repeatedly and you just continue to take the hits without throwing a counter-punch, then you are doing it right. Showing any aggression or pursuing your ex in court will likely lead the judge to see you as the aggressor and your ex as the victim. I hate saying this, but you just have to continue to take the hits.

Here is a brief overview of the rules I chose to govern my battles, which will be explained in detail following the list:

1. Live clean and blameless – Stay far away from anything that might overshadow the issues.
2. When accused of wrongdoing, wait it out and the truth will surface. Sometimes it is a gift in disguise.
3. Never underestimate your enemy.
4. Remember the Iron and the Silk.
5. Never have a conversation with your ex-wife unless it is recorded (written or audio if you are

in a one-party state; please discuss with your attorney).

6. Hang silk blossoms on the dead cherry tree.

7. Never corner your adversary, always leave hope for an escape.

8. Watch the fires burning from across the river.

9. Accept that you have control of yourself and no control of someone's response.

10. Never interrupt your enemy when they are in the process of committing a grave error.

11. When you are strong, appear weak; when you are weak, appear strong.

12. Use chaos to your advantage.

13. The greatest victory is that which requires no battle.

14. Compartmentalize your emotions when dealing with your child's mother.

15. Do not be hateful toward your ex-wife.

16. It's not about her.

17. If they ask for a cup of sand; give 'em the

    beach.

3.1 – Live clean and blameless

Ok, this should go without saying, but I am going to say it again: If there is no other rule that you follow to the letter, please pay attention to this one. If you break the law or your court order, you will not only lose custody of your child, but you might also lose your freedom.

This sounds like a no-brainer, but it becomes very difficult in some circumstances. I will give you an example:

My ex-wife had made death threats toward my son and me in the past. There had been some major friction between my son and his mother. I was dreading the fact that he was going to have to go to my ex-wife's house for the weekend and honestly, I had a pit in my stomach sending him over there. I firmly believed she posed a physical threat not only to my son, but to my life as well. That said, if I had denied her visitation, I would have been in contempt of court.

Then why did I consider breaking the court order? Well, for starters the amicus in the case told me that if I strongly believed my son's life was in danger that I should violate the order and refuse her visitation. This put me in a very tough spot; I did not sleep much that weekend. I could not afford to appear to disregard the orders of the court and feared the judge may interpret that action as sign of disrespect for the court. This would have made me appear to fit the description my ex-wife had defined for me.

In another instance, my son was freely telling me about things that went on at my ex-wife's house –

the constant drama, the fighting, the emotional abuse, the poor living conditions, etc. I could not ask him to clarify anything or grill him on details because it was not only against the court order, but it would place him further in between the crossfire of the ongoing battle.

Keep in mind that a custody battle can last years. There has been ongoing litigation for the past nine years in my case. Half of my son's life has been tied up in court. What a horrible way to have your childhood destroyed. The good news is that my son tells me over and over again he is so glad I stood up to his mom and got him out of there. That is all that matters to me.

While touring the college campus where Caleb is attending, he made quite the declaration: "Dad, had I not gotten taken from my mom's house, I would not be

38

going to college. I don't even know where I would be."

That statement made everything we have been

through completely worth it.

Anytime I made a decision, I always weighed

how it would affect my son and our relationship. I

encourage you to do the same.

3.2 – Wait it out and the truth will surface.

I cannot tell you how many times my ex-wife has accused me of wrongdoing. To be honest, the only two specific crimes that I know she has not implicated me in are the shooting of John F. Kennedy and the murder of the Lindbergh Baby; apparently everything else has been fair game.

To summarize my ex-wife's battle strategy, it has been to hurl allegations until eventually something sticks, no matter how erroneous the claims. If only 30 percent of what she accused me of were true, I would have been on the FBI's most-wanted list next to Whitey Bulger.

What is amazing is that she even filed sworn affidavits with the court detailing these allegations. One of these claims was that I had been physically abusive during our marriage and that I beat her on many occasions. I was so happy when she finally filed that as part of a sworn statement in court: Finally, she had made her claims of abuse and violence a part of the court record.

In 2003, the Office of Personnel Management performed an in-depth background investigation as part of a pre-employment security clearance process for a federal agency. They had sent a federal investigator to speak with my ex-wife about me on two separate occasions. During these interviews, there are standard questions about family violence, history of alcohol/drug abuse and any other behavior that would prevent the United States government from hiring you. They even ask, "Would you recommend that we hire

_____ to work for the United States government and carry a firearm as part of his duties?"

On both occasions, the investigator took sworn testimony from my ex-wife that not only did I not have any alcohol or drug problems, but I also had no history of family violence – and my ex-wife even recommended me for the job.

So, by changing her story years later and claiming that I used to beat her when we were married, she was actually doing me a favor. She was committing perjury, either when she testified to the background investigator or in the affidavit before the court; either way, she made it clear that she is a liar. This was a gift in disguise.

Another example of a time when I was accused of wrongdoing was when my son told school officials that I was abusive at home:

I went to my son's school to pick him up, and instead of him being outside waiting for me, I was met by a police officer who said I needed to come inside and speak with him in the office. I was lead into a conference room where the head principal, assistant principal, a school counselor and another police officer were sitting with grave looks on their faces.

I asked what was going on, and they told me about my son's report. My heart felt like it had just been run through with a knife. How is it that I have made so many sacrifices for my son only to be treated this way? Of course, I immediately knew the source of the storyline; after all, it was the same broken record that had been playing for years.

After repetitive questioning by the police, they decided to bring my son into the room and lay out his options. When they told him he could choose to go to a shelter or go home with me, my son suggested they just call his mom and she could simply come to the school to get him. The counselor informed my son their only choices were to send him to a domestic violence shelter or send him home with me.

My son said that if I would not say anything about what had happened that afternoon, he would go home with me and we could just all forget about it. Everyone at the table was gob-smacked, and it was clear that, although my son was clearly terrified, he was not afraid of me. Much later, the truth surfaced along corroborating evidence of the school's closed circuit television footage that revealed my son's mother had come up to the school and had an animated conversation with him. According to my son, his mom told him he would make a report about me being abusive at home or she would kill him. Her favorite threat has always been, "I am going to run you off of a bridge and make it look like an accident."

It has broken my heart to watch my son work through the anxiety his mother is responsible for, but I am very proud of how much he has accomplished.

3.3 – Never underestimate your enemy

I think it is accurate to say that too many times I have underestimated what my ex-wife would do in certain situations. I have learned much about her and I know to never trust her, but always to be cautious when she makes threats; you never know where they will lead.

Around 2008, my ex-wife's daughter (we'll call her Peggy, for the purposes of this discussion) called me on my cell phone while I was at work one day. Peggy was my stepdaughter when I was married to her mother. I had not seen Peggy aside from the handful of times she caught rides with Caleb and I when I picked Caleb up for visitation. Peggy was about 14 at the time, and it was clear to me she was emotionally wrecked.

46

Peggy told me about her mother's boyfriend and said he had been sexually assaulting her for over a year. Peggy went on to tell me she was calling me as a last resort because she did not know to whom else she could turn. I would have to say that Peggy and I had a pretty good trust built at that time, because I was able to get her to agree to go to the sheriff's department with me that afternoon. I left work near downtown Houston, Texas and drove out to a small town outside of Houston to take her to the police.

Once we were at the sheriff's office, a deputy trained in sexual assault cases interviewed Peggy. Soon thereafter, my ex-wife arrived with her boyfriend. There was no physical evidence of any sexual assault, so the officers had no choice but to send Peggy home with my ex-wife and the person who had been allegedly sexually assaulting for over a year. Years

47

later, I found out the alleged abuse continued until Peggy ran away from home.

My ex-wife's words to the sheriff's deputy were, "My ex-husband over there [pointing her finger] thought up this plan to try to make me look like a bad mother and it failed. But, I'm sure he'll try again." Yes, even though her daughter was allegedly a victim of rape, she could not see anything aside from her hatred of me. My ex-wife taunted me as she escorted her daughter out of the sheriff's department that day. Truly unbelievable.

Years later, Peggy got married and her husband told me of nights where she would wake up in the middle of the night screaming; the bed would be wet from sweat and then she would cry until daylight. I am no psychologist, but it is my opinion that Peggy was telling the truth about the repeated sexual assaults.

Additionally, a family member passed away in 2016 and Peggy was at the funeral with her new husband. We were speaking outside and Peggy's husband told me about how Peggy recounted some of the threats from my ex-wife. According to him, my ex-wife allegedly got in Peggy's face during an argument and said, "I let ******* rape you because you deserved it and if you f*** with me, that's what happens…"

Is my ex-wife in jail? No. Is anyone looking into any of this?

No.

Why?

Because life is not fair.

Do you remember me telling you my ex coerced my son into reporting me for abuse? I didn't see that one coming. Never let your guard down. Attacks will come when you least expect them; see the explanation of the Iron and the Silk to understand this dynamic.

As far as underestimating my son's mother, this is an area where I have suffered repeated failures. With each failure, I have had to painfully learn the same lesson – Never underestimate your enemy. But it is an easy trap to fall into. Or maybe I am just a slow learner.

In my case, my ex-wife lacks an education, cannot hold a job for any length of time and has very few friends, so it has been pretty easy to feel I am in a better position than she is. But she has proven time and again that the amount of evil she is capable of is outside the breadth of my imagination. I have learned it is best to just know she is going to bite, but not to try to set expectations on the limitation of damage she can inflict.

There have been so many attacks that were based on fabricated lies that I honestly think she might have done much better writing fiction horror books instead of focusing her hatred toward me for the past 18 years. Stephen King has nothing on this woman.

My ex-wife has threatened to run my son off of a bridge and make it look like an accident. She has threatened to run her daughter off of a bridge and make it look like an accident. She has threatened to run me off of a bridge and make it look like an accident. I have informed my family that if I die from unnatural causes, I want the back of my tombstone to read, "See, I told you she was crazy."

Most importantly, an enemy that has nothing to lose is your greatest threat. Because my ex-wife really has nothing, the worst that can happen is that she ends up with nothing. In contrast, I stood to lose everything. This was empowering to my ex-wife, and many times I lost sight of this, so I was caught by surprise.

3.4 – The Iron and the Silk

Once again, I am borrowing from Chinese warfare strategy to put a face on a concept that needs to be understood if you are dealing with an unpredictable person. Even the most unpredictable people might develop patterns of behavior over time. My son's mother did, and it helped telegraph to me when to expect something bad to happen.

"Oh look, I got a nice card in the mail from my son's mom saying Happy New Years," I would think – only to be followed by some form of legal harassment or other form of attack. I came to call this the rule of the Iron and the Silk.

In ancient China, soldiers would tie red silk sashes to the hilt of their swords. Many people have

53

mistaken these sashes to be some sort of decoration. On the contrary, these sashes are strategically placed to make the blade virtually invisible when wielded by a swordsman.

If you were standing in front of an ancient Chinese swordsman, you would be able to see the trail of the red sash, but you would not be able to anticipate where to meet the blade with a countering move. It is hard to block that which the eye cannot see, so fighting an opponent with an invisible blade proved to be very difficult.

In the same way, my son's mother has repeatedly shown kindness right before doing something utterly destructive and spiteful. While this kind of behavior may not apply in your situation, I encourage you to be watchful for these patterns so you can learn from them.

By anticipating the strike, I still felt the pain of the blow, but at least I was not taken completely by surprise.

In court, my ex-wife would talk about how she sent me a birthday card with best wishes to misdirect people about her intentions, when she was actually in the process of trying to disrupt the peace by denying visitation, making threats or otherwise wreaking havoc on everyone involved.

Regardless of what action was taken by my ex-wife, she always came back saying, "But I sent you a birthday card wishing you a happy birthday" or

55

"Christmas card", etc. In sword fighting, they call this a "Feint".

There are two types of feints in warfare, the "feint attack" and the "feint retreat". Both tactics share the same goal of using deception in order to lead the recipient to make a hasty response that puts them at a disadvantage.

This is why I think it wise to always keep the Iron and the Silk in the forefront of your mind when your ex-spouse does anything. You need to be slow and calculating in your response to avoid any action that would place you at a disadvantage. An immediate vulnerability assessment should be taken, and your reaction needs to be carefully considered prior to offering a response.

3.5 – Never have a conversation with your ex-wife unless it is recorded

Before I go any further, let me remind you that I am not an attorney and I am not here to advise you about what is legal in your state. Seek the advice of legal counsel and operate within the laws of the land you live in.

Thankfully, I live in Texas and we are a "one-party state," which basically means as long as I am a part of the conversation, I can record it.

While some people immediately think recording the conversation is solely for the purpose of catching the other party saying something bad, it is much bigger than that. Not only is a recording good to document what the other party said, but you can show what you said as well; this is more important, in my opinion. Protect yourself.

I have gone before a judge and told him my ex-wife threatened to kill me; I even played the audio. The judge's initial reaction was, "Well, maybe she was just upset."

Had the shoe been on the other foot, I am not sure the court's attitude would have been to brush it off like it was no big deal. Do I believe in an impartial judicial system? No way. If you are a father trying to get custody of your child, you will be fighting an uphill battle, I assure you. I am not only speaking of the judicial system in general, but the general public as well. This is why you should proceed with the utmost caution and always protect yourself.

If I had ever threatened to kill my child's mother, I would have gone to jail. It's a guarantee. While I have been able to avoid getting convicted on criminal charges based on false allegations, I have been tried and found guilty many times in the court of public opinion. Unfortunately, this comes with the territory.

There have been so many times when I have met people for the first time and they treated me with absolute contempt, simply because they believed the lies my son's mother spread. Get used to that discomfort; it will not go away anytime soon. Church, school activities, family functions, you name it – that awkwardness will be there.

Back when we were married, my son's mother would repeatedly hit me and then cower in the corner screaming, "Please don't hit me!!" Psycho? Yes, I believe so, but what would someone standing outside of our apartment think? This is why you need to take every step to protect yourself and not allow yourself to be dragged into their manipulation if you are dealing with someone with serious issues as I have for the past 18 years. This means that if she hits you, walk away. If she stabs you, just get away. If she shoots you, then you might have an easier time of getting custody – really it's all in how you look at it.

Cover your ass and be ready to take one for the team, because any other response will likely get you thrown in jail. I have taken my fair share of strikes, jabs and character assassinations, but here I stand.

In my case, it was not the recordings that I presented to the judge that ultimately won custody of my son: It was the fact that I stood quietly and allowed my ex-wife to dig her own hole in front of the bench. Honestly, she did all of the work; some of it I recorded and saved for later; other times, she just had to open her mouth. Again, it comes down to your perspective, but she did me a favor just about every time she started talking.

3.6 – Reverse psychology and misdirection

"Hang Silk Blossoms on the Dead Cherry Tree"

– Sun Tzu, The Art of War

When you are determining your rules of engagement, you should tailor your approach to meet the objectives you have set. Will you win on all points? No, not likely. But you need to know what is most important to you and where you are willing to compromise. Knowing from the beginning where you are able to compromise without losing at the table will help set yourself up for success. No matter what, you will end up in some kind of negotiation; be prepared.

Although I went full tilt in court to get custody, the courts are not quick to make drastic changes;

when they do, many times it is temporary to see how things change afterwards.

In my case, I was granted an Ex Parte order to take immediate custody of my son, and then my son's mother contested the Ex Parte order. In lieu of going before the judge, we came to an agreement in the hallway the following day. I had all of the eggs in the basket at the start, but I had to give up some of those eggs over time. But which ones?

I had prioritized the things that were major issues for me: the right to make educational decisions, the right to determine my son's place of residence and the right to make medical decisions. The last thing I was concerned about was money.

My son's well-being is more important to me than any price you can place, so money was never a priority for me. But, I knew money was a major flashpoint for my son's mother, so I never discounted the power of the word "money" when it came to these kinds of negotiations.

From the very beginning, I asked for child support knowing it would command her attention. Asking my ex-wife to pay child support was more like lighting the fuse on a bomb, but it helped conceal the stated goals above. Remember the word "feint"? This is how to use an "attack feint" in battle.

I wasn't asking for much, but just the idea that she would have to send me a check every month would send her into a rage. Blinded by her anger, my ex-wife rushed into the ambush I had prepared and completely missed what I was truly after – being able to look out for my son's future.

In front of my ex-wife, I continued to let money appear important to me so when it came time for negotiations, I would take a "loss" when it came to the amount of child support she would pay. I kept the core issues close to my chest and never revealed what would really hurt me. When my ex-wife thought she was winning, she was only getting what I wanted her to have.

For this type of feint to work, it must never be revealed to your opponent until after the war has been won and your child turns 18. I have kept this feint going for nine years. If your children are younger, you will have to keep your true objectives between you and your attorney to assure success applying this tactic.

Did my ex-wife ever act in a way that made me believe she was looking out for my son's best interest? No. So before you rush to judgment saying your child's mother would never act out of malice, please refer above to where I speak of never underestimating your opponent.

While some might say this is reverse psychology and it doesn't work, I have to say that it worked quite well for me. My ex skipped out of the negotiation like she had just left me unconscious on the mat; but she took nothing of any value to me. I'd call that winning in a big way.

Conceal your feelings, compartmentalize that burning emotion and only speak about your case with your attorney and close family; otherwise you will get

burned alive.

3.7 – Leave them a path of escape

"When you surround an army, leave an outlet free. Do not press a desperate foe too hard."

– Sun Tzu, The Art of War

To understand the wisdom behind this advice, you must first look back at why Sun Tzu made this statement in the first place. Sun Tzu called it "Death Ground" when an army was afforded no avenue of escape; he believed an army would fight with double or triple the spirit when faced with no alternative than victory or death. Sun Tzu was known to light dry forests on fire behind his own army to elevate their motivation to win the battle based on their own desire to survive.

I did not want to place my opponent on "Death Ground" for many obvious reasons, but mostly because an arguably bat-shit crazy ex-wife had threatened to kill me and my child. Forcing her to fight out of desperation might have had grave consequences for my son or me, so why invite this kind of evil? The words, "If I can't have him, then nobody will" still resonate in my ears. Of the many threats she has made, this is one I was very weary of hearing.

I had many pieces of evidence that, by themselves, could have gotten my ex-wife in some serious trouble with the courts; but leaving the negotiating table with a deal was much better than forcing her into the courtroom. Had we gone into a courtroom, I was concerned I might place her on death ground and invite a desperate response I would end up

regretting.

No matter what, it was clear that the court was

not going to very easily take away her visitation rights.

It is a delicate balance and, while there are some who

believe you should fire every shot you have in the fight,

I think that this is not the correct approach in a case

with someone who you believe is mentally unstable.

Do only what is necessary and allow them to leave

with the hope of escape; otherwise you might be

inviting a tragedy.

On one occasion, my ex-wife fired one of her

attorneys at the courthouse. Immediately thereafter,

her recently fired attorney asked me if she could walk

out of the courthouse with us because she felt

threatened and wanted our protection. I couldn't help

but smile on our way out, knowing this attorney had woken up that morning with a plan to destroy me and now was walking under my wing to safety. Unfortunately, it would violate attorney/client privilege to call her as a witness, but it still provided some reassurance that I was doing the right thing for my son's future.

I live in Houston, the hometown of Andrea Yates. While many people have judged her husband for not getting her help and taking his children, I said, "How exactly does that work?" If you tell someone your ex-wife is bat-shit crazy, they just nod their head and say, "Yeah, I have heard that so many times." Keep in mind; even though I was able to get custody of my son, I have had to defend custody the entire time. Nothing has happened quickly; it has taken years.

If you think organizations like Child Protective Services will help you, you might be sadly mistaken. Keep your expectations in check if CPS is involved. It has been my experience that CPS is practically worthless. They can do just as much harm as they can good.

In my case, they always sided with my son's mother and made excuses for her actions. I even provided audio recordings on my ex wife threatening to kill me and take Caleb to another country to hide him.

We had several interactions with CPS along the way and my experience has left me with a less than favorable opinion. That said, the only one who is going to stay committed to helping your child through this is you, and hopefully your friends and family. Keep that in mind when dealing with social workers or others appointed by the court to "look out for what is best for your child." My experience has been that they have no skin in the game and generally couldn't care less.

There was only one entity assigned by the court that ever really helped out and that was the amicus attorney. An Amicus is an attorney appointed by the court to look out for the best interest of the child. It is common, as in our case, that the parents split the legal fees of the amicus. Sometimes, you might get lucky like I did, but don't ever expect help from outside sources; treat it as a blessing when it occurs.

3.8 – Watch the fires burning from across the river

If you find yourself in a situation where the dynamics are very much the same as my experience, your ex-wife always has drama in her life and it seems she is always the victim. In my case, my son's mom was always having drama with the rest of her family, so there were times she was so enveloped in combat with her daughter, her sons, her mother, her aunt or other family members that she would not be fighting me at all. I took advantage of these side battles and used them as breaks to restore myself. Her constant quarreling also helped establish a pattern of deception, manipulation and pure evil.

Why cross the river to join the fight when others are accomplishing the mission for you without any effort on your part? You are best staying uninvolved and only proceeding with your attack once the enemy is weakened and tired.

Avoid getting drawn into drama that does not already involve you. Of course, if there is a defenseless child involved like Peggy, then you need to do what you can to get them the proper legal help, and then let the authorities handle it.

3.9 – You have control of yourself and no control of your ex's response

One fact you need to accept and own is that the only thing you will be able to control is yourself. People will not always respond to you the way you think they should; this is especially true when it comes to an ex-spouse.

You could do everything right and still lose. Unfortunately, this is the way it is. That said, if you do not control yourself, you are predestined for failure.

My attorney has told me I can give the impression that I am an "arrogant asshat," while my son's mother looks like the downtrodden victim. Well, she has had a lot of experience at playing the victim, and I lost sight of that a couple of times. Although I was not always appreciative of my attorney's remarks, he was only looking out for me and I needed to listen to him.

Focus on maintaining your composure in your interactions with your ex-wife. No matter what, if you yell back while she is shouting like a banshee, you will lose.

You have no control over what she hears; only what you say.

3.10 – Never interrupt your enemy when they are in the process of making a grave error

While this quote was originally attributed to Napoleon Bonaparte, it has been rewritten and polished in the past few years. Woodrow Wilson once wrote, "Never … murder a man who is committing suicide." I don't know if I could further simplify the point.

It should go without saying, but when you notice your adversary making a big mistake, let them finish that thought or action. It is easy to get wrapped up in emotions and respond immediately to attacks, but first you must analyze the long-term effect of their action.

Be slow to anger, and delay your response. This takes a lot of practice and discipline.

There are so many examples I could use here from my own experience, but like I explained earlier, my ex-wife was the star player even though she was the other team. If she was opening her mouth, then I just needed to keep mine shut. The more I realized this truth, the better life became.

This was no more evident than when it came to the audio recordings and the ramblings of an insane, angry maniac on the phone. In one instance, my ex had fired her attorney the previous day and had to find a replacement that afternoon for the next morning's hearing. Imagine the judge's surprise when one attorney begged for a hearing, he granted it and then overnight the first lawyer was replaced with an attorney who turned down the hearing. Why? After hearing the audio we were prepared to play for the judge, her new attorney was concerned she may end up in jail. My ex-wife had outright threatened to kill me and harm my son; she also was on tape accusing me of paying off the judge who was going to be hearing the case.

If you are recording a phone call and try to speak while the other person is talking, then you will be left with noise. If the other party is running their mouth and lying about you, saying horrible things, tearing down your momma, whatever – Do not interrupt them. Grant them silence and listen to what comes out of their mouth; it might be a gift.

Discovery is a pre-trial procedure during which each party obtains evidence from the other party through requests for the production of documents, answering questions known as interrogatories and depositions. If your opponent makes a strategic blunder and sends you something in discovery that is just erroneous, don't bat an eyelash. Do not telegraph to them that they are making a mistake; you will only be granting them time to correct the error. Use it to your advantage when the time is right. You will likely only be able to use it once – if you are lucky, maybe twice.

If in doubt, keep your mouth shut.

One of the greatest errors my ex-wife made in the early days of our custody battle was accusing me of being physically abusive during our marriage. Again, this turned out not to be a bad thing; it was a gift. I was very upset at the time, and my mind started spinning thinking about how I was going to counter the

81

accusation. Finally, I arrived at a clear answer: I just needed to get the sworn testimony from my background investigation that had occurred after our divorce. Alcohol, drugs and domestic violence are topics a background investigator must cover during the course of such an investigation.

Not long after our divorce, I had gone through a pre-employment background investigation for a federal law enforcement position. The Office of Personnel Management sent a federal investigator to meet with my ex-wife to take sworn testimony to help determine if I was morally fit for a clearance and be trusted to carry a firearm on behalf of the government.

Now, years later after being taken to court for custody of our son, she had fabricated stories about how I was abusive during our marriage. My ex told everyone horrible stories about me, and it really made me feel uncomfortable when people treated me like an ax murderer; all they knew is what she had told them. But who cares about the court of public opinion? The only court that matters is the one in which a judge is signing the order after reviewing evidence.

Finally, my ex-wife filed a sworn affidavit to the court accusing me of being physically abusive toward her. I was so relieved when I realized she had made this error, because I had already submitted a Freedom Of Information Act (FOIA) request to the Office of Personnel Management for the records pertaining to my background investigation. My ex-wife had telegraphed her intentions long before filing the affidavit, so I was able to anticipate her move.

In one hand, I had sworn testimony of my ex-wife telling a federal investigator I had never been abusive, had no issues that could be used for blackmail and that I was morally fit to be a federal law enforcement officer; in the other hand, I had sworn testimony under oath that she was accusing me of being physically abusive during our marriage. It was no longer a question of whether she was lying, just a matter of which time she lied under oath.

Given the circumstances, I think it is not hard to figure out in which instance she was not telling the truth. Obviously, she had plenty of motive to lie in order to try to get custody of our son back.

The sworn testimony taken by the federal investigator was one of my biggest aces, and I kept it close to my chest. It was this document that also

84

helped persuade her attorney that court was not a good option that day. To this day, I don't know if she even knows the card I was carrying; she folded before my hand was called.

3.11 – Appear weak when you are strong, and strong when you are weak

This is a concept that is very hard to put into practice. Never show your enemy where you're vulnerable to attack. Your adversary will look for your weaknesses, and attack you when and where they think you are weakest.

One of the hardest parts of planning your strategy in a custody battle is that not only do you know your adversary better than most people, the same can be said on their end, as well. They will already know many of your natural weaknesses, and this is where you will basically have to appear to be an impenetrable fortress. This means, you will need to work on yourself more than anyone else. You will have to change or you could lose the fight.

In my case, my attorney and friend, Sean Cody, was very open with me and told me where I had flaws that needed to be addressed. While it can be hard to take criticism, never underestimate the value of your closest advisors – they will be able to make observations you will be likely to miss due to your proximity to the situation.

Sean would say, "Dave, stop being a dumbass and think about this for a minute." In the immortal words of Sean Cody, "Dave, you are F---ing up!" It is rare to find a friend who will just confront you and tell you how it is, but that's exactly what I needed to hear.

One of my greatest challenges has been keeping my emotions under control. When my ex-wife called me before the holidays and wanted to renegotiate the terms of when I was going to see my son, I had a hard time not getting upset. I had already ironed out the details of holiday possession and made plans with my extended family, and then Caleb's mom would want to change everything. This was not a once or twice thing: Practically any agreement we came to would change. That makes it difficult when you are planning to go out of state to visit family.

Then she would make demand after demand on the threats of going back to court. One time I got so angry that I spiked my phone into the concrete. Well, that was stupid; it cost me $400 for a new phone, and she still did what she wanted. I accomplished nothing. My emotions have been a weakness that I have had to focus on fixing to be effective in this fight. My ex-wife knew my triggers. I needed to disarm them one by one. It was a daily process, but losing my temper only gave her more control.

When it comes to character weaknesses that need to be addressed, look to your close circle of friends you can trust, and rely on their counsel. They will be able to advise you on where you need to make improvements. It is hard to take that kind of criticism, but keep in mind it might be just as hard for them to be honest with you. You need their trust; do not lash out. Just listen and lower your defenses. I am not a poster boy for this advice, by any means. I am just blessed to have friends, family and an attorney who didn't want my stubborn ass to drown.

If you have an external weakness, you might only have to construct temporary defenses. There was a time I had to borrow money for parking at the courthouse; I was seriously that broke. Not information your enemy needs to know. Today, I laugh about it, but I assure you it was not funny at the time.

On the flip side, appearing weak when you are strong can be used to draw fire from your opponent. If you were paying attention earlier, this is called a "retreat feint." This is a great diversionary tactic that can expend much of your enemy's energy without causing you any real duress. For some reason, my ex-wife thought she could tell me my mom had said something horrible, and then call my mom and say I said something equally as horrible. She would then wait for my mom and me to have a disagreement based on her false reports. I never called her out on her futile attempts at causing discord in my family. My only response was, "Man, I can't believe my mom would talk about me like that." (This statement is true, but can be interpreted in different ways)

My mom is my rock, and there have been so many times when we called each other almost at the same time to laugh about whatever craziness my ex-wife had cooked up. Not allowing my ex to know these attacks were pointless and ineffective only meant that she spent countless hours coming up with all sorts of scenarios to try to divide us. I have no doubt this was exhausting for her, and my mom and I just sat back silently. Just smile and wave, boys; just smile and wave.

3.12 – Use chaos to your advantage

"In the midst of chaos, there is also opportunity."

– Sun Tzu, The Art of War

How you deal with chaos and pressure is going to likely bear great weight on the outcome of your case. There are a couple of things I would like to address before going further into this subject.

When things are chaotic and you feel you are being attacked on all sides, do not allow yourself to get too caught up in the anxiety of the moment. This is another trap that is easy to fall prey to, but it is another weapon that will likely be used against you.

If you are caught off guard, hold your tongue until you have time to regroup. Think before you speak

92

or act. The "fog of war" is often used to describe the confusion that can occur on the battlefield, and I think it accurately describes what can easily happen when you are surprised in a court battle. If you are ready for attack at all times and can keep your mouth shut, you should be good to go.

Being paralyzed with fear or anxiety is a sure way to concede defeat: Do not allow this to happen.

Instead, when chaos erupts, recognize this may be more of a blessing than a curse. In my experience, chaos follows in the path of my ex-wife because she is like a destroyer that roams the earth attacking anyone in her path. Then she plays the victim when people respond to her behavior. She turns on the waterworks and lures well-intentioned people in to showing her compassion. It is a cycle.

Do not get caught up in this cycle. Remember: Do not interrupt your enemy when they are in the process of making a grave error.

While your tendency in the midst of chaos might be to speak up, I urge you to hold your tongue, listen and think before speaking. When confusion is being passed around and emotions are high, it is easy to say or do something that will be used against you. Instead, wait to gather what can be used by you to further your cause.

In my case, the recipe was fairly simple: Trust no one from her circle, and do not immediately react to anything that was said. If asked a direct question, respond with "I'll think about it" or some other statement that cannot be held against you later. Or keep your mouth shut and take note of what might be

of use to you among the chaos.

3.13 – The greatest victory is that which requires no battle.

While this idea sounds like common sense, it is much harder at times to allow this to play out. There will likely be times during which you feel attacked, and there might be lies that accuse you of things you had not even begun to imagine.

I was accused by my ex-wife of paying off the judge, opposing counsel, and some random person at a medical clinic. In that string of accusations, instead of going to battle over it, I chose to not respond immediately. Allegations such as these are golden opportunities for you, but you must hold onto them like precious gems and only show them when the time is right.

In my case, I had all of these conversations recorded. I chose not to make an issue of the accusations at the time, and I did not bring them up until we were literally in the courthouse. One of my ex-wife's attorneys heard the recording about five minutes before we were to walk into the courtroom and completely changed their tune. Either the judge was going to believe I had the power of a mafia boss or it was going to be apparent to everyone that my ex-wife was delusional. Her attorney actually said, "Look guys, we both know that my client is batshit crazy," and then proceeded to look for an alternative to going into the courtroom.

Imagine if the judge had heard the recording of my ex-wife accusing him of taking bribes from me. It probably would not have been very good for her. Of course, we leveraged that for a deal that would assure victory for the day.

Choosing not to immediately react and fight a fruitless battle paid off down the road when truth was allowed to bubble to the surface. This took no energy from me; all I had to do was keep my mouth shut. Easy as pie.

3.14 – Compartmentalize your emotions when dealing with your child's mother.

One of the greatest skills you can acquire is the ability to compartmentalize your emotions and stick with strategic thought. This takes a lot of self-discipline.

The good news is, self-discipline is like a muscle: The more you use it, the stronger it becomes. Once again, I do not want to give the impression that I am a poster child for this, but compartmentalization is the goal.

In 2005, I went to New Orleans as part of a contract security force that responded after Hurricane Katrina. I dealt with a lot of angry people who would say just about anything to trigger a response.

I was lucky to have a mentor like my friend, Joe. He explained to me that in his 30-plus years in law enforcement, his method was to speak softer as people got louder. I thought this was strange advice, but very soon I discovered the wisdom of those words.

People who are trying to illicit a response by saying inflammatory things are looking for behavioral cues to let them know how effective their attempts are at getting to you. When someone is yelling in your face and you speak softly back at them, you are saying two things: 1) You don't bother me, and 2) I am the one in control here.

I got daily practice dealing with people who would yell in my face, spit at me and threaten physical violence. It was not very pleasant, but it became invaluable later. Joe's advice helped me avoid escalating a situation while maintaining control of myself.

Once I started to apply these lessons while dealing with my ex-wife, there was a major shift in the dynamic between us.

She was still hell bent on causing as much damage with her mouth, but she seemed to get further frustrated when her words slid right off of me and I did not change in my tone. If she sent me a nasty text message, I would not respond. If she called and started running off of the rails, I would just let her run her mouth.

I can't tell you the number of times, looking back, when I can now clearly see how she would attack from an angle seeking a response and I had played right into her game. The only way she exercised control over me is when I allowed her to control me.

I have been tempted to feel shame for how I have not handled situations well in the past and allowed her to control my every move. She would call me repeatedly until I would answer, so I answered my phone. I allowed her to have control. She dictated my life even though we were no longer married. She used my son as a pawn, and I fell for that.

All of these past failures are not shameful to me because they came together to teach me the lessons that propelled my son and me to victory. Had I kept my emotion out of it back then, things would have improved for my son and me much sooner.

I share this now because it is important for you to realize that years ago, I was blind to these facts too. I had many friends try to counsel me and give me great advice, but I could not see what they were talking about. They might as well have been talking to me about an army of unicorns flying across the sky riding on rainbows made of Pop-Tarts. It was unthinkable. It was my belief at the time that, while my friends had perfect intent, they did not truly understand my situation.

The reality is they knew exactly what was going on and I was just too emotionally wrapped up in it to listen to their counsel.

One of my greatest friends throughout this battle was my attorney Sean Cody. Sean had the patience of

Job and did everything he could in the best interest of Caleb. Sean has gotten frustrated with me in the past for failing to keep my emotions out of it and think rationally. Luckily for me, Sean never gave up on me and stuck close by, just like a good battle buddy.

3.15 – Do not be hateful toward your ex

I personally believe this is the hardest rule to follow at all times. There have been so many personal attacks against me and my son that it has been very hard not to harbor resentment towards my ex-wife.

Holding bitterness against your adversary in this fight will not only cloud your judgment, but your child will pick up on it. My ex-wife is full of piss and vinegar, so just being around her breeds anxiety for my son. The last thing I wanted was for him to see me bitter, and angry as well.

Yes, there were times when I was pretty angry. There were times when I thought I should pursue some kind of retribution in court. At the end of the day, however, none of those thoughts were going to benefit my son or me.

The more people witnessed both of us, it became self-evident who was the aggressor in the situation and ultimately helped me maintain custody of my son. At one point, my ex-wife had weekend visitations, and when she filed to get custody back, it resulted in her losing her visitations and only getting a four-hour visit once a month with a supervisory program.

Not only did she gain nothing, she lost ground. At times, I had to let victory come to me without pursuing it.

This is counterintuitive for me; I normally use aggressive action to defend myself and my family, but this has no place in a family court situation. Had I

acted out of spite or hate for my ex, the court wouldn't

have seen any contrast between us.

Not harboring hatred towards your ex is not a

one-time act: It is a daily struggle. I still struggle with it

from time to time, even now. One of my closest friends

urged me to pray for my ex-wife every day. At first, I

grudgingly prayed for my ex out of duty as a Christian.

Over time, God changed my heart and healed those

wounds.

Hate is like a cancer. If you allow it in your heart,

it will grow and consume you. It will poison your

relationship with your children and affect your life for

many years.

Temptations to make snide or witty comments, but I had to resist the temptation to give her any ammunition. A good example was when my ex-wife called me to tell me she had just been in a rollover accident and had hit her head really hard.

For some reason, she was asking me for advice on what she should do. I was so tempted to tell her to take a couple of aspirin and lay down for a nap. Instead, I told her that she should go to the emergency room and wished her the best.

Did she go to the emergency room? No. Come to find out, she wasn't even in a rollover accident. Once again, she had tried to illicit a response that could be used against me and failed to get anything that would help her.

3.16 – It's not about her

There have been so many times when my ex-wife made the accusation that what I was doing was only to hurt her. In reality, I was acting in what I believed to be my son's best interest.

Let's face it: Caleb had been enrolled in five schools in five years, and at the time that I originally filed for custody, he was not even enrolled in an accredited education program. I think it is safe to say something needed to be done.

My ex-wife's responses were always fueled with questions like, "Why are you doing this to me? What are you going to get out of this? Why do you hate me?" She would say, "Caleb is my blood and my body and you are ripping my heart out." Yet, she didn't care if

Caleb was not getting what he needed. She only cared about maintaining some semblance of control over everyone's lives.

Of course, my favorite argument was, "I carried that baby for nine months, and you don't know how it feels to have them ripped from you." I am not going to waste time explaining the biological answer why this should be completely ignored aside from saying these statements are placing an impossible burden on you and are only meant to illicit a negative response. I thought to myself, "So now I should feel guilty because I don't have a uterus?" If you show anger, she is winning.

No matter how many times I said it, it was never about her. The entire case was predicated on what was best for Caleb. Had I set out to attack my ex-wife out of malice or spite, I would have been filleted by the judge and sent packing.

You must keep your focus on your child/children or you will surely lose the battle before the first shot is fired. No matter what she throws in your face or what buttons she pushes, never take your eyes off of the reason you are in the fight.

If you allow the case to become about your ex and not your child, you have defeated yourself.

3.17 – If they ask for a cup of sand; give 'em the beach

Interrogatories, discovery and production are just part of the process. If there is something you think you can hide through omission, then you are dancing with the devil and asking to be held in contempt of court. This part of the process was just as stressful for me as it is for anyone else. Luckily, I have been through similar processes in the past, during which every aspect of my life was put down onto paper and combed through by professionals. But this time I had something that I was not very comfortable disclosing.

Unless your ex-wife has loads of cash, this search can be used to your advantage. I chose to send full color scans at the highest resolution I could. I used a flatbed scanner and saved each page with a unique filename. This gave them the most accurate scan I could provide, also the largest.

The other effect that it had was that full color, high-resolution files are quite large, making them cumbersome to open and sift through. By giving them a boatload of files, I knew they would have to spend more time combing through what I submitted than it took me to scan them.

Just like anyone else, I have things in my past I did not want to be used against me in court. I figured by giving them everything under the sun, my ex would either go broke paying her attorney to sift through everything or she would have to do it herself. Either outcome would be to my benefit.

Here was my dirty little secret: By the time that the custody battle was in full swing, I owed the IRS for back taxes. Had she discovered that, it could have been used against me. The reality was that I abruptly stopped working as a security contractor and, after being unemployed for about six months, took a drastic pay cut (two-thirds).

Instead of paying my taxes the minute I left contract work, I used that money to live until I got a job. Did that prove I was financially irresponsible? Maybe. I guess people will judge me based on their own priorities. I can deal with that.

My immediate priority at the time was to intervene in the direction my son's life was going, so I had to make a choice. I was going to spend my time and money trying to protect him and sort out my issues later. I made arrangements with the IRS to pay the back taxes and, while I am tempted to feel ashamed about that at times, I still believe I did the right thing given the situation. Eventually I will be paid up and my son's life will be better as a result of the immediate action I chose to take.

So, knowing the gravity of the skeleton in my closet, I am sure you can understand my trepidation at handing over my financial records.

Once we had submitted our response to the request for discovery, I didn't hear a word about taxes, back taxes or financial irresponsibility. To this day, I do not think my ex-wife's attorney took the time to sift through every single shred of paper we provided.

To be truthful, I think I would not have looked as good in court if the financial responsibility and ability to provide for my child had become an issue. Thankfully it was missed completely.

They requested tax returns, phone records, notes, audio recordings and much more. I had years of audio recordings, phone records, financial statements and other documents, but they did not put any limit on how far back they wanted them to go. I gave them everything.

In my case, giving them the entire beach when they asked for a cup of sand worked to my advantage. This might be a tactic you can discuss with your attorney.

Chapter 4 – Guidelines governing my actions with my child and others

1. Sometimes you are the man, Sometimes you are the deer.

2. Never speak poorly of your ex-wife in front of your child.

3. Apologize to your child when you wrong them.

4. If you do not know what to say or you are charged with emotion, remain silent.

5. Semper Gumby!

6. Encourage your child to seek wisdom from the counsel of others.

7. Never make a promise to your child you are not sure you can keep.

8. Never blame your child for actions that are influenced by the other parent.

9. Never give fuel to the enemy – i.e., never tell your child something you don't want your ex to know

10. Treasure hunting

The list above is simply a condensed list of what I will be covering in this chapter. Many times I found myself focused on the case and what my ex-wife was doing that I did not take a step back to listen to my friends and family. This list not only applies to how to treat your child, but how I found I needed to keep myself in check when talking with friends or family.

If you are in a custody battle, there will be times of great stress and it is easy to get upset when people try to weigh in with their thoughts. Dismissing their views may not only hurt them, but you may be missing a valuable observation that they are making.

4.1 – Sometimes you are the man; Sometimes you are the deer

I had an experience as a freshman in high school that I will never forget. I was on a trip to a state park with some friends from a campus ministry group and found myself alone in the woods at Inks Lake near Burnet, Texas. While walking alone down one of the trails, a deer appeared, and she was walking on only three legs.

The doe had one of her front legs tucked beneath its body and was sort of hobbling through the woods. I tried to approach the deer but that did not go over well, so I sat on a rock and threw tortilla chips at the deer. In case you are wondering, tortilla chips are like crack to deer; they love them. Salt and corn will never be refused by a deer.

After a short time of gaining this deer's trust, I started dropping the tortilla chips closer and closer to my feet. As the deer inched its way closer, I was able to see the needle from a cactus stuck between the hooves of the deer. The area was swollen and oozing, and I had no doubt it was infected.

I am sure had this been in the wild, the deer would have never allowed this, but in the state park the wildlife are known to be a bit more used to human interaction. After almost exhausting the entire bag of chips, this deer was standing right in front of me, and I reached out slowly to pet the deer.

The deer was licking the salt from my fingers and hands. All was well until I reached around the deer's neck and grabbed it by the leg.

I struggled to remove the cactus needle. Not only was I getting kicked in the legs and chest by the hind legs of this deer, I also got head-butted. That deer fought me for several minutes as I continued to try to get the needle out of her hoof. Finally, I was able to remove the needle and the deer gave me one swift kick to the gut as she darted away from me.

The deer turned back about 50 feet or so and bowed her head as she tapped her wounded foot on the ground. Then, she shot through the woods like a cannonball.

I was sore, bruised and cut, but I felt great. Looking back, I wonder why I didn't just call a park ranger and let him help the deer, but I was a freshman in high school who was doing what I could to help.

The following morning, that deer was at my camp and readily walked up to me looking for more tortilla chips. I had earned its trust, and although I had caused the deer pain and fear, later it had realized I was only trying to help.

I have used this story many times to illustrate the custody battle for my son. There have been times when my son was the deer and I was just trying to get a thorn out, but the only gratitude I seemed to get at the time was getting kicked in the face.

Unfortunately, when I let frustration get the best of me while talking with close friends or family about my custody issues, I acted more like the deer when they were only trying to help me. I eventually realized I had been speaking out of frustration towards my allies; much like the deer, I had been kicking them in the face the whole time.

The battle you will be fighting can affect relationships with friends and family members. I urge you to remember this illustration when speaking with others and look at their hearts before you speak. This will save you pain and will help maintain the respect and support you will need to prevail in this conquest.

I have been very blessed to have a family that supports me, friends who have stood by my side and a girlfriend who was totally committed to seeing my son

heal from his wounds.

4.2 – Never speak poorly of your ex in front of your child

After years of hearing piss and vinegar from his mom's mouth, Caleb knows exactly what his mom's character is. He also has observed how I have dealt with his mother. The second part is the most important function as a single parent. You must give your child contrast so they know the difference between you and the other parent.

You already know what your child is going to learn from the other parent; all you can control is what they learn from you. Always keep this in mind when speaking to your children. If you are negative and angry all of the time, you are not likely to have any kind of close relationship with your child.

On the flip side, if you treat your child with respect and do not disrespect the other parent in front of them, you will earn their respect. You want them to see contrast between the two of you, and this is one area in which you can make a night-and-day difference in what they witness.

Let's face it: I could not care less what my ex-wife thinks about me. Her opinions mean nothing to me, and I don't care if she thinks I am the best dad in the world or the biggest tyrant since Joseph Stalin. At the end of the day, I know she and I are likely not going to be able to meet on common ground about much of anything. And that is fine with me.

But, if my son were to say he did not respect me or love me, it would rip my heart open. This is why I make a constant effort not to speak poorly of my ex-wife in front of my son. Why would I even want to bring her up in discussion? The very thought of his mother gives him anxiety.

When my son first came to live with me, he did not know me very well. I was not allowed to see him on a regular basis, and our visits were always attached to stipulations his mother would dictate. She rarely followed the court orders and he never had enough time to get an idea of who I am. Most of what my son believed about me came from what he had heard from his mother.

I was very fortunate to have a girlfriend my son quickly learned to trust. My son would not tell me things for fear that I would go into a wild temper-filled rage, start killing villagers and begin practicing a scorched earth policy or something. Again, much of what my son believed about me was a lie, but it was all he really knew, so coming to live with me was a huge adjustment.

My son told me at one point that he used to be afraid of me because his mom told him I was a terrorist and a trained killer who was prone to violence at the slightest provocation. She told him I had paid off judges, attorneys and even had the police paid off so I was never arrested. To hear this now, sounds ridiculous and almost funny, but I assure you it is no laughing matter when you have a 10-year-old son who is terrified that you even exist.

I would argue that this type of reality-altering projection from the other parent is very destructive and should be considered a form of child abuse. But, it is also very easy to make comments that will lead your child to think similar things about the other parent. The main point here is this: You can only control your actions and your words. Your child will one day realize the score and come to their own conclusions. If you try to force them into thinking a certain way, they will likely fight you, and that will only add to the emotional toll this will take on you and your child. Focus on what is best for your child and they will figure out the rest.

Life might not be fair, but you have to treat your children fairly. Where else will they learn how to act?

4.3 – Apologize when you are wrong

If I had to list the number of times I have made mistakes being a parent, it would take five years to write this book. Some of those mistakes involved how I conducted myself either around my son or directly towards him.

If you were the only person who could teach your child/children how to act, would you act differently than you already do? There have been times when I said something before thinking or have forgot about something my son felt important.

In those instances, I believe the only thing a real man can do is to approach your child/children, apologize and tell them directly that what you did was wrong. I would also add that I believe it is in poor form

130

to ask them to forgive you: This might place them in a position in which they feel forced to respond in a way that is pleasing to you. They will forgive you when they see your heart. The only way to teach respect is to give respect.

My son has had a life full of empty promises, so I have only used the phrase "I promise" on several occasions. Unfortunately, I promised to take my son to an event that ended up being in conflict with another commitment I had scheduled. I completely forgot about promising to take him to that event, and although he was not outwardly upset, I sensed I had greatly disappointed him.

I broke my word, and it really hurt to know that I had let him down. I apologized and he accepted my apology. The world might not be fair, but I want to be fair and honest towards my son. If there is one thing I

want him to remember about me when I am gone, it is

that I treated him with respect like a man.

4.4 – If you do not know what to say, remain silent.

While this statement seems very simple, the application has been an uphill battle for me. If it helps, carry a Miranda card with yourself and remind yourself that you have the right to remain silent and anything you say or do will used against you.

I cannot tell you the number of times I was told something inflammatory in an attempt to trigger a response. It is your response to these tactics that will dictate the direction of the battle. Sometimes, the best response is silence.

Sometimes, your child will exhibit the behavior of the other parent and resort to using their tactics. It's what they have been taught, and it might be the only way they know how to deal with a situation.

I will freely admit I have struggled with the above rule many times, and that in many cases I failed to uphold it.

A great example is how I responded to the court-appointed service that was to supervise Caleb's visitations with his mother. I entered the program with many misconceptions:

1. I thought the people at the program would look out for my son's interest.

2. I thought the program would treat my son with dignity and trust.

3. I thought the people at the program would not allow themselves to be manipulated by my ex-wife.

We had been ordered to go to supervised visitation at our temporary orders hearing, but it was all contingent on my ex-wife's responsibility to initiate the visits. Almost a year after our temporary orders were entered with the court, I got a call from the program's director telling me my son's mother had provided them with the court order and had initiated the registration process. She emailed me a packet and told me the first visit was going to be in three days.

Caleb was very anxious about the visit and wanted to speak with the director to address some of his concerns. During that conversation, he was told that if his anxiety reached a level for which he wanted to leave, he could terminate the visit at any time. I had to fill out a bunch of paperwork that included my social security number, as well as other personal information.

Within the first month, the program had an employee walk off with my paperwork, and then they asked for me to send them another copy. I was outraged that my social security number had been carelessly handled. In addition to that, what the director had told my son about leaving any time he felt uncomfortable had not been communicated to the staff working the first visitation.

I spoke to the director of the program regarding what she had said about allowing my son to leave when he felt that his anxiety was too high, and she apologized saying that she would make sure to clearly communicate this to her staff for future visits. At the next visit, the director was present, yet they still forced my son to stay until long after he was in tears and screaming to leave.

136

Over time, I came to believe the group was full of women who have a disdain for men. They did not seem to care that I was the custodial parent. They would defend my son's mom whenever she started crying, no matter what the circumstances were. She manipulated them constantly, and then they reportedly gave feedback to the courts indicating she was a victim. The sad part is, the only victim here was my son, and they never defended Caleb or were truthful with him.

When it became clear to me that the program staff had lied to my son and me, my attorney advised me to just let it go. According to him, I was asking to stir up a hornet's nest that could cause issues if I were to raise any further objections to their incompetence. I should have listened to Sean.

137

Instead, I sent a scathing email to the program director expressing my disgust at their actions. At this point, I did not see how the visitation program was going to be constructive for my son; they had lost our confidence. As it turns out, while the program is appointed by the court to supervise visitation, there is apparently no oversight. I have called the state Attorney General's Office, checked for licensing and gotten nowhere. Apparently the program staff can say whatever they want, do whatever they want and you either play ball with them or they will crucify you in court.

The director emailed me, instructing us not to come back to the program until we had gone to court again. So, for the next couple of months, we did not attend the visitations. Then I got an invitation from my ex-wife (some people call this a subpoena) with a motion to find me in contempt of court. I was following the instructions of the program the court had ordered us to attend, and now it appeared that they were colluding with my ex-wife to burn us down. Unbelievable.

If I had to do things over, I would listen to my attorney and just keep my mouth shut. Luckily, in our situation, the program was not involved until Caleb was turning 17 years old, so there was not much that was likely to change before his 18th birthday.

If you have to deal with court-appointed organizations such as this, treat them no differently than you would if you were handling an angry pit viper. Use caution and never call them out for their incompetence. You have no power and they know it;

they will abuse you if they want and might try to destroy you if they feel attacked.

One of the workers at the program called my son "manipulative" and a "horrible person" during one of the visits, so I am sure you can understand why I reacted with immediate words. Looking back, it was still a mistake. I should have just accepted that they are court appointed and have unchecked power over our lives.

Is life fair? No. Accept it and drive on. Sometimes silence is the better part of valor. It would have greatly helped me to take the advice of my attorney. Had this happened sooner in our custody experience, it could have had a much greater impact on the outcome.

4.5 – Semper Gumby!

Most people are familiar with mission statements, mottos and other taglines companies use to keep their folks motivated. These prepared statements give their people something to fall back on when times are hard.

Here are some examples:

- United States Marine Corps – Semper Fidelis (Always Faithful)
- Fujitsu – The possibilities are infinite
- United States Coast Guard – Semper Paratus (Always Prepared)
- Ford Motor Company – Quality is job one
- United States Navy – Honor, Courage, Commitment

- United States Air Force – Above All

- Apple Computer – Think Different

- United States Army – This We'll Defend

My motto throughout this process has been "Semper Gumby" (Always Flexible). Things will not always go the way you expect, and during those times you must keep your eye on the overall objective.

There will be setbacks and there will be storms, but you must stay true to the course you have determined for yourself.

I once got a fortune cookie that had a quote from Confucius that read: "The green reed which bends in the wind is stronger than the mighty oak that breaks in the storm." While I am not advocating you go searching for wisdom in random baked goods, I do think the point is well made.

When things do not go as you would wish, stay true to your roots, but move with the motion or you might get broken.

A great example of this was when we went to mediation the first time. While I had to compromise on some points I was not too excited about, I was able to claim victory in the areas I had determined had top priority. I realize this is all a part of compromising at the negotiation table, but when it involves your child's future, it is very difficult to allow for flexibility.

Had we not negotiated in mediation and gone back into the courtroom, it could have been anybody's ballgame. Contrary to the allegations made by my ex-wife, I had not paid off the judge and I was facing an

uphill battle as a father in not only demonstrating to the

court why it was best for my son to live with me but

getting the court to agree to my point of view.

4.6 – Encourage your child to seek wisdom from the counsel of others

Part of my daily life is seeking out the counsel of those I respect before making difficult decisions. If there is one place your child can learn this, it will be from you.

I highly recommend speaking to your child about this directly and ask them to identify those who you seek for counsel. I did this exercise with my son, and it allowed him a window into my world and how I go about making critical decisions.

I asked, "Son, when I am having tough times and need advice, where do I go?" Of course, he was able to list a couple people instantly, but as he thought about it, he started naming people a bit more removed from the situation.

Then I asked Caleb to whom he turned for counsel. My son basically told me it was me, my mom and his other grandmother. I followed up by asking to whom he could talk outside of the family dynamic to get an outsider's perspective.

This was foreign territory for him, and I ended up having to help him make a list of people to whom he might want to talk. I also told him that if he ever needed to speak with someone regarding what he was going through, I would respect his privacy and not try to dictate how that conversation went.

I have been taking my son to a counselor for years to deal with the wounds inflicted upon him. I firmly believe that a key element to success in life is knowing how to identify good sources of advice. In addition to his counselor, I wanted to show Caleb he could ask people he knew and trusted.

The short list my son was able to produce was his youth minister, a friend's dad, one of our neighbors and a teacher at school.

Branching out and talking to others about the issues he was facing allowed my son to get a broader view of what he was dealing with. Basically, it helped him gain perspective no one individual could have provided. I am grateful to all of those who helped Caleb during those times; it taught him an important lesson about asking for advice.

4.7 – Never make a promise to your child you are not sure you can keep

One of the goals I set early on was never to make empty promises to my son. It is much better to be realistic with your children than to create expectations you cannot meet.

My son's mother broke so many commitments that my son did not place any value on a promise. I believe promises are very important and have a place in any relationship. A promise is a sacred thing that must be kept.

If promises mean nothing, then why make them at all? No matter what, I wanted my son to respect the fact that I never broke a promise to him. Of course, I mentioned earlier how I am not perfect and broke a promise to him; but I did not establish a pattern of that behavior. When I am dead and gone, my son might not agree with all I have done, but he will at least respect me for treating him fairly and keeping my word.

I cannot emphasize to you the value of making a promise that requires sacrifice and pushing yourself to make good on that promise. There have been times when I made a promise thinking it was completely realistic but became very difficult to accomplish as the situation changed.

For instance, when I told my son that if he was selected to go study in Germany, I would make sure he could go. When my son made it through the selection process, I was excited and immediately filled with the

149

questions concerning how I was going to pay for him to get there.

The simplest answer I have is that I was bound and determined to send him to Germany, even if it was the last thing I did. We ate lots of peanut butter-and-jelly sandwiches to put money aside.

Another obstacle was the fact that my ex-wife was completely against him going anywhere. She threatened me on more than one occasion that if I sent our son out of the country, she would find a way to "make me pay."

With her past history of creating a living hell on earth for Caleb, I wanted to avoid giving her the opportunity to ruin his study abroad program experience. Caleb beat me to the punch by asking me to keep his trip a secret. Smart kid.

I was concerned that if she found out when he was scheduled to fly out, she might call TSA and report that I had trained him as a terrorist and he might have a bomb with him. While that sounds outrageous to a sane person like you or me, this is commonplace behavior for my ex-wife.

When I was in college, she tried many times to get me to drop out of school. "Get a job like a real man," she would say. After her attempts failed at getting me to quit school, she called the Financial Aid Office and told them I was not attending classes that semester but had received grant money and she "didn't want to get into trouble."

The Financial Aid Office immediately dropped my classes and put a hold on me. I was unable to get my classes back and had to take what was leftover. This cost me an extra semester in college, so if I seem a bit gun-shy, I do have my reasons.

So, the night before Caleb's flight to Germany, I whisked him away to a hotel north of the airport where nobody would know where we were. I did not want to even allow for the opportunity for his mother to stop us from leaving.

The morning of my son's flight, I saw a twinkle in his eye I rarely have seen throughout the years; he was beaming with excitement. As I walked him into the airport, my son hugged me and reminded me he didn't want me to say a word about his whereabouts until his plane landed in Germany.

I had made a promise to my son that he would get to study in Germany and I followed through with it. I never allowed his mother the opportunity to stop him from going.

I was blessed with some extra work on the side that made me enough money for me to go to Germany for about 10 days, as well. I got to explore some of Europe with my son, and he served as my translator. The best day of this trip was when we visited Salzburg, Austria. We were on a regimented tour of Germany and Austria, but I had talked to the tour director and received his approval to just hang out in Salzburg for the day.

Caleb and I explored Salzburg together and had a blast. It was a very special time for us, and I will always cherish those memories. My prayer is that you

will be able to do similar things with your children and

share similar experiences.

4.8 – Never blame your child for actions that are influenced by the other parent.

In the introduction, I mentioned that, at one point, my son told school officials I was physically abusive at home and depriving him of food. Imagine my surprise when I showed up at his school to pick him up and was greeted by a police officer.

I was questioned for a couple hours by not only by the police but the head principal, assistant principal and a counselor. At the end of their questioning, they brought my son in and asked him if he wanted to go to a shelter or go home with me. My son suggested they could just call his mom and she could come get him. Once the school officials made it clear that going home with his mother was not an option, my son opted to go

155

home with me as long as I did not speak of this incident when we got home.

Honestly, I felt like my heart had been ripped from my chest and stabbed a thousand times. But, deep down, I knew this was not something my son would have done on his own volition.

Later, it came out that my ex-wife had gone to the school that day and without signing in as a guest, confronted Caleb. Her cover story was that she was there to give him "lunch money," but it was clear to anyone familiar with the situation that something more than that had transpired.

My son apologized to me and I have forgiven him, but to this day, I think some of that guilt still haunts him. We have talked about it in group sessions with his counselor, and I have made it clear to my son that I forgive him and do not blame him for what happened.

I have to say that out, of all things my ex-wife has done, this was the one time when I actually contemplated giving up. I felt abandoned and betrayed by my son. I could have easily lost my job and my freedom. I had to ask myself, "Is this really worth it if Caleb is going to turn around and wound me so deeply?" The answer was yes, of course. I love him no matter what, and I had faith that he would see the big picture eventually.

I am relieved I did not hold him accountable for what had happened that day. Caleb was acting out of fear for his life and had I punished him for what he told the school, it would have left him all alone without

157

anyone to fight for him – only fueling his depression. Had I been placed in similar circumstances, I probably would have acted in a similar fashion. Caleb was just trying to survive.

Because of situations like this, even years later, my son is still wounded. The wound I still carry is the knowledge that he has not fully recovered, but every day I see him making strides towards a very bright future.

Had I said things out of anger and pain that night, I would still regret it to this day – and all it would have done was cause further injury to my son. Please, if you find yourself in a similar situation, find a way to not react towards your child.

No matter how hard you try, no matter the sacrifices you make, inevitably you are likely to face the same challenge. I would suggest making a commitment to yourself that you will not lash out at your child.

Of course, once the truth surfaced, I subpoenaed some of the people who were in in the room for my interrogation. Only one of them seemed to have any recollection of the events that transpired and, to this day, I am grateful for his candidness in the deposition.

Do not be surprised when outsiders want to stay uninvolved and use the old phrase, "I do not recall." At times it will seem as if your ex can do or say anything without consequence, but you just have to continue walking the line.

159

The damage inflicted on my son is an onion for him and his mother to peel one day. I am blessed to have a son who is an amazing young man. I almost said kid, but he is an adult now and I treasure the time we have had together.

I could not be more proud of my son for all he has overcome, and I am confident he will see continued success on the path he is taking. I wish the same for your children.

4.9 – Do not give the enemy fuel

"Remove the firewood from under the cooking pot."

– Ancient Chinese Stratagem

It has been my experience that information has been the driving force behind the power my son's mother has used in the past. No matter how benign the information may be at first, she would twist it into a piercing dagger and try to plant it in my chest.

Caleb has told me of times where his mother would ask a question and, based on his response, craft a follow up question to dig deeper. Most of these interrogations would be under the ruse of having a great time, not even under hostile circumstances. But, once she had what she needed, she would set out on the warpath with her schemes and plans. It is too bad she was not sent to Afghanistan to help find Osama Bin Laden. I believe she would have located him in less than a year.

To put it lightly, I had to run my house and my actions with counter-intelligence in the forefront of my mind. I know you must be thinking at this point that I need to remove my tinfoil hat, but let me ask you a question: Have you ever been around someone who is not happy unless everyone else around them is completely miserable? If so, listen up.

Do not tell your child anything you would not tell your ex. Period. End of story. Otherwise, you are asking your child to keep secrets, and this is a burden that ends up ruining their childhood. Not only do they have to be concerned with angering you if the other parent finds out whatever this information is, they might also feel guilty about not telling the other parent.

My son knew of some of the plans my ex-wife had in store for me, but I never interrogated him to get that information. Once he bragged that he knew something was coming, almost as if he wanted to bait me into questioning him or maybe just warn me, but I knew deep in my heart where this attitude was coming from. Putting myself in his shoes, I would hate to be caught in the middle like that. It is a no-win situation, and you need to be the parent who allows your child to escape that constant torment.

It was not until my son was 16 years old that he and I were ever successful at keeping anything from his mother. For those who care to judge me for keeping secrets, go ahead, but when information is used as ammunition, it's best to keep information to a minimum. At times, it felt like I had to run active countermeasures against an intelligence agency in my own home, but it paid off.

My ex-wife would ask my son about my work, what time I left, what time I got home, what restaurants I frequented, what I did on the weekends when he was not with me, how much our rent cost, what cable service did we have, etc. It was ridiculous. At some point, you have to draw the line.

Not long after my son came to live with me, he said he wanted to learn German and one day go to Germany to work on his language skills. I wasn't just excited about this prospect; I was ecstatic. Finally, my son had expressed something he wanted to do, not because he thought I or his mother would like it; but because it was something that he wanted to experience. I promised him then I would do whatever I needed to do to help him reach that goal.

His sophomore year in high school, Caleb applied to the study abroad program and I told his mother about him wanting to go to Germany. Her immediate reaction was to tell me that if I got my son a passport, she would take me to court and under no circumstances was she going to allow him to go to Germany.

My son applied anyway but was not chosen for the trip that summer. He was very disappointed and his mother said, "Well, I don't understand: I told your dad that you could go. Why didn't you get picked? I guess you weren't good enough." Words like this cut my son's heart open; it was no different than twisting the knife after someone is already wounded.

Once again, never underestimate your opponent. You would think that when a child has experienced failure, a mother would not view it as her own victory. Luckily for us, Caleb's mother did. She commented to him that she had "no problem with him getting his passport." I sent her a text to verify that she was okay with him having a passport, and she said it was fine. In some sick world, she saw Caleb's failed attempt at going to Germany on the exchange program as a personal victory for herself, but I had it in writing that I had her permission to get the passport. Awesome!

The following year, my son applied for the German Exchange program and he was readily accepted. What had also changed is that my son was now 16 years old, so I was not required to obtain the signature of his mother before applying for his passport. My son said he felt his mom would stop at nothing to prevent him from going to Europe. As I mentioned earlier, Caleb and I were in agreement that his mother had a pattern of trying to derail anything she could in order to use it as a means of bargaining for something.

So, by my son's suggestion, we made his Germany plans in complete secrecy. No social media, no talking about it with lots of people at church – only close friends and family knew he was going. Caleb wanted me to wait until he was wheels-down in Frankfurt to even let her know he was going to study in Germany. Now that is just sad, but it is a fact.

Information is a weapon. Respect it. Protect it. Do not burden your child with knowing something that he or she might get interrogated about in the future.

This rule applies to anything open source such as Facebook, Twitter, School Newsletters, etc. If you do not want your ex to know something, keep it to yourself. It is only when your child is much older and has been burned so many times by his or her mom that they will see your wisdom. When the time is right, they will come to the conclusion that less is more and follow your example.

Mastering this craft takes discipline and lots of patience. There will be many times children will not use good judgment and talk about something. It is through the fallout of what gets destroyed that they will learn to keep their mouths shut. By the same token, you can do a lot of damage by getting upset with them for speaking about something they shouldn't. You need to place yourself in their shoes and stand back to let them get burned; they will catch on. Had I just let things take their course sooner, my son likely would have learned a whole lot faster.

Did I tell my son in advance that he was going to Florida for a week when he was in the 6th grade? No. I literally told him he was going with my girlfriend to Florida the day before they left. Why? Again, you have to think of the consequences if his mother called the police stating that my girlfriend had kidnapped him and was taking him out of state.

I was going to be in Kenya on a church mission trip. With me being overseas without access to a phone, this could have created a very sticky situation had there been problems with my girlfriend taking Caleb to Florida.

Another example of how I had to modify my actions to avoid providing fuel for my ex-wife is how I chose to discipline Caleb when he was a child. I was raised believing "spare the rod, spoil the child." The issue was, however, if I spanked my child my ex-wife might use that fact to try to perpetuate the idea that I was a violent and abusive person.

No matter what, you must avoid providing fuel for the enemy; otherwise you might lose.

4.10 – Treasure hunting

There have been a couple instances during which I have come across things that did not jump off of the page at first glance, but after further review I couldn't believe I had missed it. Without these small gems, I am not sure how my case would have panned out. Quite frankly, some of them helped dictate the outcome.

One of the greatest examples was when I was reviewing the psychological study that had been ordered by the court. As I mentioned earlier, my ex-wife has established a pattern of threatening people that she will "run them off of a bridge and make it look like an accident."

When asked about these threats during the psychological assessment, her response was quoted verbatim. The first couple of times I read through the epically long psychological profile, I totally missed the significance of her answer.

Let me ask you a question: How much will your attorney charge to read a 20-plus page document multiple times to sift through the details? What about an attorney appointed by the court? The answer is pretty simple; You are the one who has the most skin in the game, so you need to do your own sifting and scanning.

While reading our psychological profile for the third time, I zeroed in on my ex-wife's response to the question about the threats she had made and the words just jumped off of the page.

172

"I kind of feel like I'm run out of town and did nothing wrong. I didn't threaten to kill any of us. I love my Jeep; I don't want to crash it." – page 25 of the psychological profile

I thought to myself, how did I miss this? I read further, and on the same page she was quoted as saying:

"[The amicus] doesn't care because he is running around on his wife…" – page 25 of the Psychological Profile

Had I missed these gems, they would not have been part of our case. What was really funny is that the amicus in our case was not even married, so it just helped establish a pattern of my ex-wife fabricating lies to defer blame.

There will be times when all this information runs together. Therefore, review your documents over and over so you do not miss out on anything important. If your opponent has read this book and is employing the "if they ask for a cup of sand, give 'em the beach" strategy, then you will just have to suck it up and set aside time to look through the information meticulously.

I was blessed to have people close to me who shared in the treasure hunting experience; some of them found things I did not, and their input was invaluable.

Chapter 5. – Technology

Technology helped me greatly with regards to getting custody of my son. The fun part of technology is that it is always changing, but that presents some unique problems when incorporating this into a book. Instead of writing tutorials on how to use a specific product or service, I will stick with more of an overview and point out some products many people may not know exist.

When I discuss recording devices, I have to make it clear that I live in a one-party-state, which means I am permitted to record a conversation as long as I am part of it. If you plan on recording your interactions with your ex-wife, please talk to your legal counsel to ensure you follow your state and local laws.

I think we can both agree that walking into courtroom

presenting evidence you have obtained illegally is

probably going to be a bad hand to play at the table.

5.1 – Telephone pickup mic

One of the greatest tools I used in my journey was the telephone pickup mic. This is nothing more than an earbud with a microphone inside that connects to a portable audio recorder. When you take a phone call, you naturally hold the phone to your ear and the microphone picks up the caller's voice from the receiver, as well as your voice. This type of microphone can easily be found online. I recommend buying two units, as they have a tendency to get left behind sometimes. Nothing is worse than forgetting the microphone at the office and coming home only to get a phone call you need to record. In those instances, it is best to let the call go to voicemail and call back when you have your microphone ready. Buy two; you'll thank me.

5.2 – MP3 recording device

MP3 recording devices are relatively inexpensive these days and are widely available from any office supply or electronics store. Having an audio recorder with you at all times is extremely helpful. I suggest keeping one in the car, the office and at home. You never know when you will need it, but it's also not something that is a whole lot of fun to carry around all day, so buy multiples.

From the very beginning, I decided I would only copy from the audio recorders, but I would never delete any files. This way, if there was any question about the integrity of the recordings, I could provide the original recording device should an expert witness be called to try to invalidate any of my recordings. While this seems a bit extreme, it was a cost effective way to mitigate this type of potential attack on my evidence by just buying another voice recorder once it was full. Chain of custody of evidence never became a real issue in our proceedings, so this never really took the spotlight; however, maintaining the original recordings on those devices gave me some peace of mind.

When I speak of chain of custody, it is a very important concept to understand. Chain of custody refers to how evidence is handled from the time it is collected until the time it is presented in court in order to maintain the integrity of the evidence. If doubt can be cast on whether the evidence has been tampered with, that evidence will likely be thrown out.

A good example of chain of custody would be when you see police collecting evidence and putting it into separate plastic bags. This assures that there will be no cross contamination of the collected evidence.

What you typically don't see on TV is that evidence is

logged into a storage facility and anyone with access

to that evidence will have to be tracked on the record

as well.

A family court battle is not a murder trial, but the

same concepts apply with regards to any evidence you

collect. It needs to tracked and kept in its original form,

if at all possible, to assure that the evidence is in the

same condition when collected as when it is presented

to the court.

5.3 – Text messages

Many people nowadays know you can easily take screenshots of text messages, but those can be easily manipulated. I encourage you to find a program that will recover text messages straight from your phone.

All one has to do to fake a screenshot of a text message is have access to a second phone and save that contact as "whatever name you want." Create both sides of the conversation, take photos and – voila – you have a completely fabricated set of text messages that appear at first glance to be legitimate.

This is the argument that can be used against your screenshots of text messages. Screenshots do not prove anything about what number they came from. Again, screenshots are good, but in my opinion, inadequate when it comes to being used as evidence in court. You need the metadata from the phone with the actual messages, timestamps and sender information.

5.4 – Structuring your data with the future in mind

When I started recording conversations, retrieving text messages and saving emails I did not have a good strategy for how I was going to keep track of all of it. As time started to stack up, I developed a naming convention that allowed easy reference for my data.

This sounds a whole lot more ominous than it really was, but I should have thought about what it was going to be like in five years looking at all of my audio recordings trying to find something specific.

I used a program that allowed me to cut sound bytes from each recording. I assure you that even if a judge allows recordings to be played in court, he only wants the cliff notes version. Playing an 8-minute long conversation is not likely to go over well, but if you can present 30 seconds, they might allow it.

The issue I quickly ran into was how to keep track of all of these audio clips. My recording device would name a file something like "A_044.mp3." That does you no good when looking back over hundreds of files years from now.

The naming convention I used helped me keep time, date and content in some sort of fashion to allow for easy reference. Here is an example of what I came up with:

- 20160528_0900hrs_1Full Conversation_ A_044.mp3

- 20160528_0900hrs_Paid off the Judge_ A_044.mp3

- 20091115_1835hrs_Leaving the Country_ A_056.mp3

- 20080316_1755hrs_Surprise on your birthday_ A_068.mp3

Each one of the dummy files above gives me useful information that allows me easy reference. Here is a quick overview of the naming convention that I chose:

_YearMonthDate_Time_Summary_OriginalFileName_

- YearMonthDate – October 31, 2016 would be "20161031"

- Time – I always used 24 hour time to track events and avoid the confusion of am or pm.

- Summary – Keywords related to the conversation

- OriginalFileName – The original filename of the recording on the actual device should the integrity of the recording ever come into question.

If you use this system to organize your data, you can sort files alphabetically and they will then be listed in chronological order. Trust me, this will pay off down the road. I have more than eight years of audio recordings, so having all of them noted with a system like this makes life much easier when looking for something specific. The keywords in the descriptions allow you to search for the file.

By putting a "1" in front of full conversations, the full audio recording of the conversation will always be listed first, followed by the sound bytes from that conversation.

Chapter 6. – Faith, family and friends

Without a shadow of a doubt, I would not have been successful without my faith, my family and my friends.

There were countless times when those around me have pulled me to my feet. I cannot emphasize how critical these components are going to be along the journey. While you might not be able to choose your family, you can choose your friends. I have been blessed with both a wonderful family and some pretty amazing friends.

6.1 – Faith

Towards the end of 2012, Caleb was losing weight and not eating well. I took him to his pediatrician, who made some dietary suggestions. By early 2013, my son was still struggling with his appetite. Caleb would sit down at a meal and after only a few bites, he would leave the table and eventually throw up.

This was the same behavior I had witnessed Caleb exhibit after getting phone calls from his mother in the past. It was as if she could remotely detonate him, causing him to socially withdraw, followed by complaints of a headache and ultimately nausea and vomiting.

I took Caleb to see a counselor and was hopeful I could seek help, but my ex-wife told the counselor that another counselor was already seeing Caleb and ethically she should not work with my son.

It was very frustrating to have someone being an obstacle to my ability to get my son help. Over time, Caleb began to favor one leg and was starting to limp. I asked him if he thought we needed to get it checked out, and he kept telling me that he thought it was growing pains.

In February 2013, I went on an overseas trip and, upon my return, it was obvious my son had a serious medical issue. He was limping around, and there was obvious swelling behind his knee. I was very concerned and took him to an orthopedic specialist to see what was going on. My ex-wife told me she was calling her attorney because I could not just decide to go to a doctor without her consent. My ex had me served with a motion to modify child custody the morning I had returned from my trip, and she was in full warpath mode. Instead of being glad that I was taking him for medical treatment, she responded with threats to get an injunction against me.

After a couple of X-rays, the specialist told us he was sending us to a bone center the following day. When we arrived at the bone center, more images were taken and the doctor sat down with us to tell us what he thought was going on.

"Your son appears to have cancer," he said. I went numb and heard very little after those words. My son's leg had gotten so bad he could hardly support his own weight. The doctor explained that the dull pain, low-grade fever at night and weight loss all pointed towards two possibilities – Ewing's Sarcoma or Osteosarcoma. The doctor made a call to M.D. Anderson to get us in to see an oncologist so we could aggressively address my son's medical condition.

I remember sneaking a peek at my son in the rearview mirror as I drove home thinking to myself, "My son has cancer." I was understandably a wreck. I watched my mother fight cancer when I was in the eighth grade and hearing the word "cancer" sent a wave of panic through me. While I maintained a somewhat stoic outward appearance, my heart just wanted to explode.

Not only do I have some unstable, hate-filled woman trying to ruin my son's life, now he might be taken from us both.

I remember looking into the mirror the next morning and my complexion just looked grey. I felt as if my life was being smashed from all sides. In front of my son, I was strong and full of optimism, but then I would go to some place of privacy and pour my heart out to God. I was terrified for my son.

For the next three weeks, we spent every day at M.D. Anderson going through medical tests all day. My ex-wife was there too and would fuel my son's anxiety, causing him further discomfort. I felt powerless to stop her. The head of the Osteo-Oncology department told us she suspected it was likely Ewing's Sarcoma. I am not going to get into the mortality rates of Ewing's Sarcoma here, but let's just say that it is a very tough diagnosis, especially if it has spread. I was mortified. My heart was being ripped apart piece by piece.

One night I needed to purge my emotions, so I went into the backyard. It was the only place I could get away for some privacy and not be heard by Caleb. As his father, I felt I needed to show him leadership and courage to avoid crushing his spirit. Those times when I had to purge my emotions, I would literally fall on my face and talk to God, begging for my son's life.

On that particular night, it was cold and raining outside; I didn't care, my body was so warm that I had steam rolling off of my skin. I was praying and begging God to spare my son's life, offering up whatever I could in exchange for his life – even my own.

Then, I heard the Lord speak to my heart and I was dumbfounded. God said, "First of all, he is my child and I have placed him in your hands only for the time that I have determined; second, I sent my son to die for you, so you need to check yourself at the door before coming to speak to me."

These were not the words of comfort I was looking for, but I was not going to argue. I shut up and went back inside to go to bed. The next morning, I had a completely different perspective on everything, and I had a peace in my heart. It was clear to me that God was in control. I just needed to be obedient and have faith that it would work out for his glory.

The following week, I got a phone call from the doctor at M.D. Anderson Cancer Center: My son did not have Cancer! Up to this point, all signs pointed to Ewing's Sarcoma, and they had even scheduled us for a class for parents regarding chemotherapy. The doctors had determined my son actually had a very aggressive MRSA infection destroying the bone.

While it took multiple surgeries and weeks in the hospital, my son was alive and I was so relieved. It was through this experience that God reminded me of what was truly important and that He was in control.

Throughout this entire experience, I have relied greatly on my faith that no matter what happened, it was part of God's plan. The hard part for me has always been having the faith to trust God and not lean on my own understanding.

Before walking into court, I would pray for God's wisdom and guidance as well as self-control. There is a verse in Psalms I refer to as the "Warrior's Prayer." I would meditate on this verse while deployed as a security contractor, but it has become one of my

favorite passages from the Bible. I have kept this

passage close to my heart, and anytime I feel

overwhelmed it helps bring peace to my soul. I

encourage you to read this passage and meditate on

its meaning when you are facing any battle:

PSALM 91
New International Version

Whoever dwells in the shelter of the Most High
  will rest in the shadow of the Almighty.
I will say of the LORD, "He is my refuge and my
fortress,
  my God, in whom I trust."
 Surely he will save you
  from the fowler's snare
  and from the deadly pestilence.
He will cover you with his feathers,
  and under his wings you will find refuge;
  his faithfulness will be your shield and rampart.
You will not fear the terror of night,
  nor the arrow that flies by day,
nor the pestilence that stalks in the darkness,

nor the plague that destroys at midday.
A thousand may fall at your side,
  ten thousand at your right hand,
  but it will not come near you.
You will only observe with your eyes
  and see the punishment of the wicked.
If you say, "The LORD is my refuge,"
  and you make the Most High your dwelling,
no harm will overtake you,
  no disaster will come near your tent.
For he will command his angels concerning you
  to guard you in all your ways;
they will lift you up in their hands,
  so that you will not strike your foot against a stone.
You will tread on the lion and the cobra;
  you will trample the great lion and the serpent.
"Because he loves me," says the LORD, "I will rescue
him;
  I will protect him, for he acknowledges my name.
He will call on me, and I will answer him;
  I will be with him in trouble,
  I will deliver him and honor him.
With long life I will satisfy him
  and show him my salvation."

6.2 – Family

I have been blessed with a wonderful family. My mom is one of the toughest ladies I have ever known. I watched as my mom fought stomach cancer. There were many times I went to school in the eighth grade not knowing whether my mom would be dead or alive when I got home.

I witnessed firsthand as cancer squeezed the life out of my mom's body; yet she continued to fight back. I can remember hearing the IV pump whining downstairs as I cried myself to sleep thinking she was going to die, but not knowing when.

When all hope seemed lost, my mother would pray and leave her worries with God. My mother never feared death; she just embraced life.

198

My mom has now been in remission for more than 25 years. She has been my rock and always stood beside me during this fight. There have been plenty of times when my mom has extended a hand to pull me to the surface when I felt I was drowning.

My brother and my sister-in law have been equally supportive and encouraging. The great thing about my brother is that he and I are very different. Whereas I might want to charge into a situation head first, my brother is much more precise and calculating. I guess that is why he is not only a police officer but also an attorney. It has helped me immensely to have my brother there to give me advice and counsel when I needed it most. Not only could he give me his legal perspective, but my brother was there to give me spiritual guidance, as well.

There have been plenty of times where my mom and my brother would tell me things they saw that I needed to change. It was their honesty and love that sharpened me into a blade ready for war. You need people who will call you out when you are making a mistake. I am grateful to have both of them.

6.3 – Friends

It goes without saying that it helps to have friends along the way that will stand by your side. I cannot count the times I have received encouragement from friends. While my name has been the one on the court orders, this has been a group effort.

As I mentioned earlier, my greatest battle buddy throughout this ordeal has been my friend Sean Cody. Sean has never been afraid to tell me, "Dave, don't be a dumbass! Listen to me." I need friends like that, and to have him fight next to me in the trenches has been a real blessing.

The only reason I can conclude that Sean has stuck close by to see this through is that he is a true friend. Throughout this ordeal, I have struggled financially, and Sean has never made a major issue out of money. Sean only wanted to see victory. Sean has been there to protect me against countless attacks and has provided the wisdom I needed on many occasions.

Another great friend and ally for me through this battle has been my employers. One day at work, the company founder's wife told me to have no fear when I went to court. She went on to say she knew that I was doing the right thing for Caleb and that I had their support. Her words of encouragement were delivered just at the right time. I was headed to a hearing the following day and I was not sure what outcome to expect.

The owners of the company for which I work have been there for Caleb and me all along the way. Despite the fact that my court battle took me out of the office on many occasions and, at times, affected my work performance, they stood by me.

When Caleb was sick, he missed his class trip to Washington, D.C. The owner's wife called me one night to check on how Caleb was doing, and I told her the only thing Caleb was truly worried about was not being able to go on his trip. She told me to tell Caleb that when he was better she would make sure that he got to go to Washington, D.C.

A few years later, she and her husband not only sent us to Washington, D.C., but they flew us up there in their private jet. What a blessing to work for people who value my son so much they would do something so special.

That experience was a turning point in Caleb's life. During the trip to Washington, D.C., I told Caleb I would go wherever he wanted to go in the city. Caleb planned out our days and I planned out our nights. We would go to visit the museums and sights he wanted to see by day; at night, he would accompany me while I took pictures. We bonded so much during that time. In addition to both of us having a great time, Caleb's confidence received a huge boost.

I will forever be grateful to my company's owners for the kindness and love they have shown for Caleb and me over the years. Our Washington, D.C. trip was the first of many adventures Caleb and I have shared together. It was as if they had breathed life back into my son's soul and made him realize that life has much more in store for him.

Of course, my closest supporter throughout all of this was my girlfriend, Karen. No matter what I was facing, she did whatever was necessary to ensure I was set up for success. There was a time when she drove an hour and a half a day to take Caleb to the school that had been a condition of the custody agreement. Without her, I do not know how I would have been able to keep pace with the demands of the agreement in those early days.

Of all people, my girlfriend was never afraid to give me her opinion, even when she knew it was going to stir emotions I wanted to just lay at rest. She was also my closest confidant and sounding board. No matter what I shared, she always listened and gave me sugar-free feedback. I cannot stress the importance of this partnership. If you have a significant other or spouse, they need to be onboard with you all the way.

Chapter 7 – Parting thoughts

The experience of being caught in the middle of a nasty, years-long custody battle has been taxing on Caleb. I have seen him deal with great bouts of depression and sadness. Caleb's pain has been hard to watch, because as his father, I wanted to relieve his pain – yet I was partly to blame for it. Now that Caleb is older, he has a greater understanding and appreciation for everything we have endured together. This fire has forged us together like Damascus steel.

Looking back on this experience, I would say we did well enough. There are many areas in which I would have done something different, but that's life. I am not going to get tied up with the "coulda, shoulda, woulda's" that plagues everyone after a battle.

I have great hopes for Caleb's future, and I look forward to what is yet to be. It is my sincere hope that sharing these experiences has given you some perspective and maybe some ideas on how to improve your own circumstances.

72220252R00126

Made in the USA
Columbia, SC
29 August 2019